T0022629

ROSETTA PROBE

A Robot's Mission to Catch a Comet

Robert Snedden

PowerKiDS press™

NEW YORK

Published in 2017 by **The Rosen Publishing Group**
29 East 21st Street, New York, NY 10010

Produced for Rosen by Calcium

Editors for Calcium: Sarah Eason and Harriet McGregor
Designers for Calcium: Jennie Child
Picture researcher: Rachel Blount

Picture credits: Cover: Getty Images: European Space Agency (Rosetta image), Thinkstock: Pixtum (top banner), Shutterstock: Andrey_Kuzmin (metal plate), Thinkstock: -strizh- (back cover illustration); Inside: ESA: Christophe Carreau 17, 29, CIVA/Philae/ESA Rosetta 14-15, ESA/ATG medialab; Comet image:ESA/Rosetta/NavCam 19, ESA/CNES/ARIANESPACE-Service Optique CSG, 2004 13, ESA/Rosetta/MPS for OSIRIS Team MPS/UPD/LAM/IAA/SSO/INTA/UPM/DASP/IDA 20, 26-27, ESA/Rosetta/NavCam – (CC BY-SA IGO 3.0) 25, ESA/Rosetta/Philae/CIVA 23; NASA: ESA 9, JPL-Caltech 7, JPL/ESA 10; Shutterstock: Valerio Pardi 5.

CATALOGING-IN-PUBLICATION DATA
Names: Snedden, Robert.
Title: Rosetta Probe: a robot's mission to catch a comet / Robert Snedden.
Description: New York : Powerkids Press, 2017. | Series: Robots exploring space | Includes index.
Identifiers: ISBN 9781508151340 (pbk.) | ISBN 9781508151289 (library bound) |
    ISBN 9781508151173 (6 pack)
Subjects: LCSH: Comets--Juvenile literature. | Space probes--Juvenile literature.
Classification: LCC QB721.S64 2017 | DDC 523.6--dc23

Manufactured in the United States of America
CPSIA Compliance Information: Batch #BS16PK. For Further Information contact Rosen Publishing, New York, New York at 1-800-237-9932

CONTENTS

Hairy Stars

The people of ancient Greece called **comets** *aster kmetes*, which means "hairy stars." For centuries people thought that comets flew through Earth's **atmosphere** and were the cause of natural disasters, or signaled upcoming problems, such as war or famine.

Comet Chaser

For a long time astronomers have dreamed of taking a closer look at fascinating comets. In 1985, a group of European space scientists began talking about a plan to visit a comet. They knew that it would be too far to send an astronaut, so they decided their comet explorer would have to be a **robot**. Over the next few years, the *Rosetta* mission, Europe's comet chaser, began to take shape.

Astronomers today believe that comets are leftover fragments from the formation of the solar system about 4.6 billion years ago. *Rosetta's* main mission was to gain knowledge about how the solar system began by examining the makeup of a comet.

Comets are composed of water ice, dust, and rocks, and frozen gases, such as carbon dioxide and methane. Comets mostly come from two regions of the solar system: the Kuiper Belt and the **Oort cloud**.

The main body of a comet, called its **nucleus**, is actually quite small, just a few miles across. However, as the comet moves closer to the sun, the ice and gases vaporize, or become gases, and form a cloud called a coma around the nucleus. A dust "tail," often more than 620,000 miles (1 million km) long, also forms.

SPACE DISCOVERY

ENGLISH ASTRONOMER EDMUND HALLEY (1656–1742) INVESTIGATED PAST RECORDS OF COMETS. HE CALCULATED THAT A COMET THAT HAD BEEN SEEN IN 1531, 1607, AND BY HIMSELF IN 1682, WAS THE SAME COMET COMING AROUND AGAIN AND AGAIN ON A REGULAR **ORBIT** AROUND THE SUN. HE PREDICTED THAT IT WOULD BE VISIBLE ONCE MORE IN 1758. HALLEY WAS PROVED RIGHT, AND THE COMET WAS NAMED AFTER HIM.

A comet can be spectacular sight in the night sky. This is comet Hale-Bopp, which was seen in 1997.

First Flypasts

The *Rosetta* mission was given the go-ahead in November 1993. *Rosetta* was not the first or the only space **probe** to travel to a comet. Other robot explorers have visited comets too, but *Rosetta*'s mission was special. It would not simply fly past the comet at high speed, it would also go into orbit around it and send down a lander to land on the comet. Scientists and engineers from 14 European countries and from the United States came together to build this unique robot spacecraft.

Giotto

Launched on July 2, 1985, *Giotto* was the first European deep space mission. On March 13, 1986, it flew past the nucleus of Halley's Comet at a distance of less than 375 miles (600 km). It sent back the closest images of a comet ever seen, up until then. The pictures beamed back to Earth showed a black, potato-shaped object firing jets of gas and dust into space. On July 10, 1992, *Giotto* became the first spacecraft to visit two comets, passing within 125 miles (200 km) of Comet Grigg-Skjellerup.

Stardust

The National Aeronautics and Space Administration's (NASA's) *Stardust* mission was launched on February 7, 1999. The task of this robot explorer was to travel into the cloud of ice and dust surrounding Comet Wild 2. On January 2, 2004, it flew within 150 miles (240 km) of the comet's nucleus and gathered comet dust **particles**. On January 15, 2006, *Stardust*'s sample return capsule parachuted back to Earth.

The *Stardust* probe was the first mission to capture a sample from a comet's tail and return it to Earth.

Deep Impact

The *Deep Impact* probe left Earth on January 12, 2005. When the spacecraft drew near Comet Tempel 1 on July 3, 2005, it separated into two sections: Impactor and Flyby. The main Flyby section returned images and **data** to Earth, while the Impactor was set on a deliberate high-speed collision course with the comet. The impact left a 490-feet (150 m) wide crater that threw out debris. The main spacecraft analyzed this debris to gain knowledge about the substances inside the comet.

SPACE FIRST

WHEN SCIENTISTS EXAMINED THE SAMPLES RETURNED BY STARDUST THEY WERE SURPRISED TO FIND THAT SOME OF THE MATERIALS IN THE COMET MUST HAVE BEEN FORMED CLOSE TO THE SUN BILLIONS OF YEARS AGO, IN THE EARLIEST DAYS OF THE SOLAR SYSTEM.

Rosetta: Comet Orbiter

Rosetta is like a large, rectangular aluminum box. It weighs about 3.3 tons (3 mt) and has enormous wings. The scientific instruments that Rosetta uses to do its research are mounted on the top of the 9-feet (2.8 m) long box. On one side of the **orbiter** is the 7-feet (2.2 m) diameter communications **antenna** that Rosetta uses to contact Earth. The side opposite the antenna is where the Philae lander is attached for the long journey from Earth to the comet.

Cutting-Edge Technology

Rosetta's "wings" are actually two **solar panels**. Rosetta's "wingspan" is 105 feet (32 m) from tip to tip, with each wing consisting of five panels. The total area of the panels is 344 square feet (32 sq m). Each wing can be turned to capture the maximum amount of sunlight.

Rosetta's solar cells are based on a completely new technology, called Low-intensity Low Temperature Cells. Rosetta is the first space probe to travel beyond the main **asteroid** belt toward Jupiter relying only on solar cells to provide its power.

SPACE FIRST

ROSETTA WAS THE FIRST SPACECRAFT TO GO INTO ORBIT AROUND A COMET. HALF THE LAUNCH WEIGHT OF THE SPACECRAFT WAS THE FUEL IT NEEDED FOR ITS THRUSTERS TO ALLOW IT TO MAKE THIS DIFFICULT MANEUVER.

The new solar cells are so efficient that they will allow *Rosetta* to operate in deep space where the levels of sunlight are just 4 percent of those on Earth.

Pointing in the Right Direction

Rosetta has been designed so that when it is in orbit around Comet 67P/Churyumov-Gerasimenko, the information-gathering scientific instruments almost always point toward the comet. At the same time, the communications antenna and the solar panels point toward the sun and Earth.

    Rosetta's **propulsion system** was crucial to the mission's success. A vertical thrust tube in the center of the spacecraft provides the propulsion for primary maneuvers, such as matching speed with the comet. In addition, the orbiter has 24 smaller thrusters for making little adjustments to *Rosetta's* position in space.

Rosetta's huge solar panels were carefully checked before launch.

Comet Lander

Several European countries, including Germany, France, and Great Britain, were involved in designing and building the *Philae* comet lander. The German Aerospace Research Institute was in overall control of the project.

Box-shaped *Philae* was constructed from carbon fiber with a coating of aluminum and is just 3.3 feet (1 m) across and 2.6 feet (80 cm) high. It is equipped to perform 9 experiments on the surface of the comet, including a drill to take samples from beneath the surface. Some of the instruments were stored beneath a hood covered with solar cells to provide *Philae* with the power it needed to operate on the comet.

This artist's impression shows little *Philae* on its descent toward the comet's surface.

Legs for Landing

Philae's three legs were kept folded while it was attached to *Rosetta*. Once released from the main spacecraft, the legs opened out as it descended toward Comet 67P/Churyumov–Gerasimenko. The legs were designed to cushion the impact of landing and hopefully prevent *Philae* from bouncing. *Philae's* legs were able to rotate and lift the probe so it would be able to right itself if it landed awkwardly.

The lander had no rockets with which to slow its descent or steer. In fact, a thruster on top of *Philae* was meant to push the probe on to the surface of the comet. On touchdown, *Philae* was to fire a harpoon into the comet to anchor itself. The comet's gravity (pulling force) is so weak that scientists feared that *Philae* might drift back off into space again.

Once on the surface, *Philae* could use its antenna to "talk" to *Rosetta* in orbit around the comet. *Rosetta* would then use its more powerful communication system to transmit *Philae's* findings to the scientists waiting back on Earth.

SPACE FIRST

PHILAE WAS THE FIRST PROBE DESIGNED TO MAKE A SOFT LANDING ON THE SURFACE OF A COMET. SCIENTISTS HAD TO MAKE THEIR PLANS WITHOUT KNOWING WHAT CONDITIONS ON THE COMET WOULD BE LIKE.

A Change of Mission

Mission planners made a list of possible comet targets for *Rosetta*. The flight through space was going to last 10 years and cover hundreds of millions of miles, and at the end of it *Rosetta* had to meet with a comet at exactly the right time, at the right speed, and in the right place.

In 2002, construction and testing of *Rosetta* was complete. Its target was Comet 46P/Wirtanen. Launch timing was vital to the success of the mission. *Rosetta* would have to launch some time within the two weeks after January 13, 2003.

Failure to Launch

Rosetta was to be propelled into space by an Ariane 5 rocket, but on December 12, 2002, disaster struck. A new version of the rocket failed three minutes after liftoff and was destroyed. All launches of the Ariane 5 were canceled. There was no way now that *Rosetta* could reach Comet 46P/Wirtanen. The mission planners instead chose Comet 67P/Churyumov–Gerasimenko. A new course was plotted for the new target, and *Rosetta* was soon ready to go.

On Their Way

On March 2, 2004, *Rosetta*, with *Philae* firmly attached, was launched into space by the now safe-to-use Ariane 5. After spending a short time in a **parking orbit** around Earth, it fired its main engine and headed off into the outer solar system.

A powerful Ariane 5 rocket launched the 6,610 pound (3,000 kg) *Rosetta* into space.

SPACE DISCOVERY

COMET 67P/CHURYUMOV-GERASIMENKO WAS FIRST DISCOVERED IN 1969. IT IS NAMED FOR RUSSIAN ASTRONOMERS KLIM CHURYUMOV AND SVETLANA GERASIMENKO, WHO SPOTTED IT WHILE CARRYING OUT A COMET SURVEY. IT IS A REGULAR VISITOR TO THE INNER SOLAR SYSTEM, ORBITING THE SUN ONCE EVERY 6.5 YEARS BETWEEN THE ORBITS OF JUPITER AND EARTH.

No existing rocket can send a large spacecraft like *Rosetta* directly to its target. To save fuel, *Rosetta* had to bounce around the inner solar system like a "cosmic billiard ball" on its 10-year journey. It gained speed from close **flybys** of Mars and Earth. In total, *Rosetta* would travel a distance of 4 billion miles (6.4 billion km) to reach its target.

Power Problems

Deep space missions prior to *Rosetta*, such as the *Voyager* probes and the *Cassini-Huygens* mission to Saturn, had used American nuclear battery technology for power. NASA was not involved with the early planning of *Rosetta*, so the European Space Agency (ESA) had to come up with another solution. Powerful new solar panels were developed that would work far from the sun, out near the orbit of Jupiter. The engineers also had to make sure that *Rosetta* was neither too cold in the outer solar system nor too hot as it approached the sun.

Slingshots

A year after launch, *Rosetta* made a short return visit home, as it made the first of three speed-boosting **gravity assist** flybys of Earth. It would come again in 2007 and 2009.

Before *Rosetta*'s 2007 encounter with Earth, it used the gravity of the planet Mars to change course. This was a risky thing to do as *Rosetta* would pass just 155 miles (250 km) above the Martian surface. To make things even more difficult, *Rosetta* would be traveling through the shadow of Mars, during which time the spacecraft's solar panels would not produce power. The mission controllers put *Rosetta* into standby mode to save energy. Fortunately, the maneuver worked perfectly and *Rosetta* was soon heading toward Earth again for another speed boost. This would send it out toward the asteroid belt between Mars and Jupiter and its encounter with an asteroid called 2867 Šteins the following year.

SPACE FIRST

MARINER 10 WAS THE FIRST PROBE TO USE A GRAVITY ASSIST, MAKING A CLOSE APPROACH TO VENUS AND USING THAT PLANET'S GRAVITY TO SEND IT ON ITS WAY TO MERCURY IN 1974.

Asteroid Flybys

On its way to 67P, *Rosetta* had close encounters with the asteroids 2867 Šteins and 21 Lutetia. *Rosetta* made its closest approach to Šteins on September 5, 2008, shooting past at a distance of about 500 miles (800 km). For a month before this, *Rosetta* had been taking photographs of Šteins. This allowed scientists back on Earth to calculate the asteroid's orbit.

To get the best results possible from the flyby, *Rosetta* had to be pushed to the limits of its design. Mission controllers made it perform a series of rapid flips and changes in position. As it flew by the asteroid, *Rosetta*'s onboard navigation cameras kept it pointed in the right direction. For the whole encounter, the asteroid was kept in full view of *Rosetta*'s imaging instruments.

Šteins Revealed

Rosetta's observations provided information that would have been impossible to get from Earth. Šteins was accurately measured at 4.14 miles (6.67 km) in length. Many craters could be seen on the surface, including a huge crater about 1.2 miles (2 km) wide at Šteins' south pole.

Following the Šteins encounter, *Rosetta* had a long journey back to Earth for its third and final speed boost in November 2009. Now it headed back into deep space for a meeting with the asteroid Lutetia.

Lutetia Encounter

Rosetta sped past Lutetia on July 10, 2010, passing at a distance of around 1,970 miles (3,170 km). Lutetia is much larger than Šteins, measuring 75 miles (121 km) long. There were still years of journey time ahead before *Rosetta* reached 67P. This far from the sun, the solar panels could not generate enough power to keep all of *Rosetta*'s systems running. It was time for *Rosetta* to go to sleep.

SPACE FIRST

ROSETTA'S CONTROLLERS WERE ABLE TO USE THE ENCOUNTER WITH ŠTEINS TO TEST THE CRAFT'S SYSTEMS, PARTICULARLY THE NAVIGATIONAL SYSTEMS. THEY THEN FELT CONFIDENT IN ITS ABILITIES FOR THE APPROACH TO THE COMET.

Rendezvous with 67P

Rosetta began its **hibernation** in June 2011. During its time asleep, the probe reached its maximum distance from Earth, about 621 million miles (1,000 million km). It would be 31 months before Earth heard from *Rosetta* again.

Wake-Up Call

On January 20, 2014, controllers on Earth waited for *Rosetta*'s built-in alarm clock to "wake up" the spacecraft. First, *Rosetta* warmed up its navigational instruments, checked its position in space, then aimed its antenna at Earth to announce that the mission was okay.

In mid-March, *Rosetta* took its first proper look at Comet 67P. *Rosetta*'s course corrections to catch this small, fast-moving object would have to be carried out with pinpoint accuracy.

To Catch a Comet

As *Rosetta* approached the comet, it began to brake. As 67P grew closer, a problem emerged. The comet was an odd shape. Figuring out how to orbit and land on this object was going to be difficult.

The final arrival maneuver took place on August 6, 2014. *Rosetta* was about 62 miles (100 km) from the comet. The flight team steered a careful course toward the comet. On September 10, 2014, more than 10 years after it had left Earth, *Rosetta* went into orbit 19 miles (30 km) above the surface of the comet.

SPACE FIRST

NO SOLAR POWERED CRAFT HAS EVER TRAVELED AS FAR FROM THE SUN AS *ROSETTA*. BEFORE REACHING 67P IT WAS IN HIBERNATION WITH ALL BUT THE MOST ESSENTIAL SYSTEMS POWERED DOWN.

Philae separates from *Rosetta* and begins its descent toward the surface of Comet 67P.

First Touchdown

Rosetta began mapping the surface of 67P, searching for a suitable landing site for *Philae*. Controllers on Earth carefully examined the images set back by *Rosetta*, looking for a good landing target for *Philae*. To be sure of success they wanted a flat area about 1,650 feet (500 m) across, but they could see no such place on the comet. They decided that a region given the name Agilkia looked like the best to land that they were going to find.

On November 11, a signal was sent to power up *Philae*. As the little robot lander came to life, the controllers at the German

These images show *Philae*'s descent. In the top left square you can see the marks *Philae* left when it bounced.

touchdown point

before

taken at 15:43

taken at 15:18

15:23

15:19

space agency discovered that there was a problem with the thruster that was meant to push *Philae* down onto the surface of the comet. For a while the controllers did not know whether the mission should even go ahead. However, they decided to proceed, and on November 12, 2014, the lander was released 13.5 miles (21.8 km) above the surface of the comet and began its slow descent. For 7 hours it made its long, unpowered **free fall** toward 67P, drawn gently down by the comet's weak gravity.

Disaster?

Finally, *Philae* made contact, but things quickly went wrong. Not only had the landing thruster failed to fire, the harpoon that should have anchored the lander to the surface did not work either. *Philae* bounced back from the comet. The lander traveled about 0.6 miles (1 km) before it landed again, nearly 2 hours later. Once more, it rebounded from the surface, this time staying up for 7 minutes before it came to rest 9 hours after release from *Rosetta*.

67P was so far from Earth that it took almost 30 minutes for a signal to travel from *Rosetta* to the mission controllers. No one knew what had happened to the lander: its location was unknown and it was not known whether it had landed upright.

Philae Lost and Found

Back on Earth, worried controllers tried to make sense of the data that was reaching them from *Rosetta*. A signal had been received that indicated that *Philae* had made contact with the comet, but further signals seem to suggest that the craft was still rotating. The only explanation was that *Philae* had bounced off the comet and back into space.

Finally, the mission controllers figured out that the lander had come to rest, but had landed awkwardly, possibly in a **crevasse**. There, it would be hidden from sunlight and unable to collect enough solar power to recharge its batteries. *Philae* had just 54 hours of power left in its batteries. Mission control had to make a decision about which of *Philae*'s experiments they could run. It was decided that they might not use the drill as this could tip the lander over if it was not in a stable position.

Success Against the Odds

Luckily, *Philae* was able to operate every one of its instruments, even the drill, before power ran out. By the time the signal was lost on November 15, *Philae* had streamed back all of its scientific discoveries to Earth via *Rosetta*. Then *Philae* fell silent. The scientists were overjoyed by its success under such difficult circumstances.

Meantime, Comet 67P's orbit was bringing it ever closer to the sun. On June 13, after seven months in hibernation, *Philae* gathered sufficient energy to contact Earth again. This first contact

This image of the comet's surface was sent back from *Philae*. One of the robot's legs is circled.

Philae

lasted just 85 seconds. The mission controllers waited for more news from 67P. Contact was made again on June 19, and several more times in June and July, during which *Philae* returned more information to Earth. After this, *Philae* lost touch once more. The mission controllers still hope to hear from it again before the end of the mission in September 2016.

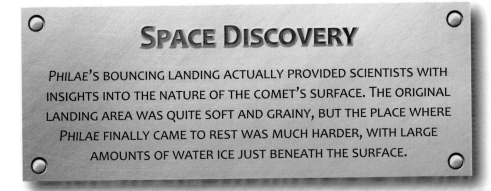

SPACE DISCOVERY

PHILAE'S BOUNCING LANDING ACTUALLY PROVIDED SCIENTISTS WITH INSIGHTS INTO THE NATURE OF THE COMET'S SURFACE. THE ORIGINAL LANDING AREA WAS QUITE SOFT AND GRAINY, BUT THE PLACE WHERE PHILAE FINALLY CAME TO REST WAS MUCH HARDER, WITH LARGE AMOUNTS OF WATER ICE JUST BENEATH THE SURFACE.

Approaching the Sun

One of the aims of the *Rosetta* mission was to observe how the comet changed as it made its closest approach to the sun.

Growing Activity

As 67P's orbit brought it closer to the sun, the increasing solar energy began to warm up the ice frozen in its interior. As comet ice warms, it turns directly into vapor and pours from the comet as jets of gas and dust. It is these jets of material that form the comet's coma, a fuzzy "cloud" that can extend for thousands of miles into space.

In the weeks leading up to the comet's closest approach to the sun, mission control told *Rosetta* to move into a higher orbit, gradually moving it out to 186 miles (300 km) above the comet. This was to reduce the chance of dust causing problems with the probe's sensitive navigation instruments.

Around June 2015, *Rosetta* scientists began noticing sometimes spectacular changes in the surface features of the comet as it became more and more active.

SPACE FIRST

ROSETTA WAS THE FIRST SPACECRAFT TO CLOSELY OBSERVE A COMET AS IT APPROACHED THE SUN.

Rosetta took this image of jets of gas and dust shooting from Comet 67P as it got closer to the sun.

The closest point to the sun that an object in the solar system reaches in its orbit is called **perihelion**. Comet 67P reached that point on August 13, 2015, around 116 million miles (186 million km) from the sun. This is about one-and-a-quarter times the distance that Earth orbits the sun.

A Wider View

About one month after perihelion, *Rosetta* began a journey that would take it 930 miles (1,500 km) from the comet. This was done so that the probe could get a wider look at the coma developing around 67P. Burning a thruster for a fraction of a second was enough to send *Rosetta* on its way. A similar return burn at the beginning of October brought *Rosetta* back to within 310 miles (500 km) of the comet, where it continued to observe activity. By November, as the comet grew quieter, *Rosetta* began to get close enough to pick up signals from *Philae*, should there be any.

Comet Science

Rosetta has made many discoveries about the composition of Comet 67P. It has discovered a water-ice cycle on 67P, in which water escapes into space from the comet as vapor and is replaced by ice from beneath the surface. Water ice on or just below the surface turns to vapor when that part of the comet is in sunlight, and this gas flows out into space. As the comet spins away from the sun, the surface grows dark, like night falling on Earth, and cools down again. As this happens, water ice moves up from inside the comet to the surface, and forms a thin icy layer that evaporates into space the next time that part of the comet faces the sun.

Researchers examining data sent back by *Philae* have found evidence of **molecules** that are sometimes known as the chemical building blocks of life. This is the first time molecules of this kind have been found on the surface of a comet. Some scientists have suggested that life on Earth got its start billions of years ago when comets crashed into the planet, bringing these chemicals with them.

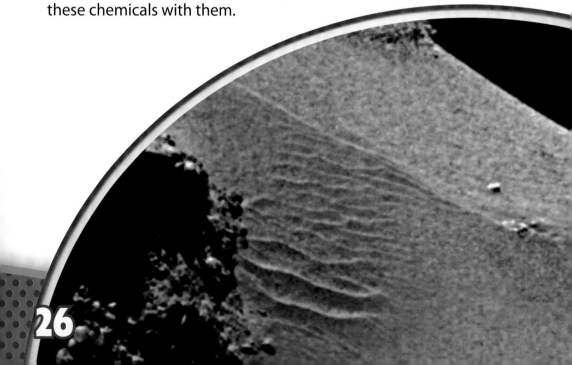

Mystery Ripples

Comet 67P's northern half has a number of dunes and ripples similar to markings found on Earth, Mars, and Venus. The mystery is that 67P does not have the dense atmosphere or high gravity that cause these features to form on the planets. One possible explanation is that gases rushing out from the interior of the comet into space could cause the rippling effect seen on the surface of the comet. So far, though, this is just guesswork.

SPACE DISCOVERY

ONE OF THE MOST EXCITING OF ROSETTA'S DISCOVERIES WAS THE PRESENCE OF OXYGEN MOLECULES ESCAPING FROM INSIDE THE COMET. THIS SURPRISING FIND SUGGESTS THAT OXYGEN WAS SOMEHOW TRAPPED INSIDE THE COMET WHEN IT FORMED BILLIONS OF YEARS AGO.

Rosetta found some strange markings on 67P, such as these ripples and dust streams.

What Next?

Rosetta's mission is due to end in September 2016, possibly with an attempted landing on the surface of 67P. Before this, the team will perform some new and riskier investigations, including flights across the night-side of the comet to collect dust samples ejected into space.

Temperatures fall as the comet's orbit takes it farther from the sun, out beyond the orbit of Mars. By the end of January 2016, Philae's temperature will have dropped below –60 degrees Fahrenheit (–51 °C), too cold for it to continue working.

The increasing distance from the sun creates problems for Rosetta too. The amount of sunlight reaching its solar panels will lessen, so there will not be enough power to operate all of its instruments at the same time.

End of Mission

The Rosetta team has decided that Rosetta's final weeks will be spent making closer and closer approaches to 67P's surface. Researchers could learn a lot by studying the comet's coma close-up and making detailed observations of how the comet's surface has changed after its approach to the sun.

At the end of its mission, Rosetta will begin its final slow descent toward the surface of 67P, gathering scientific data all the way down until it lands on the surface of the comet. As Rosetta joins Philae on the surface of Comet 67P, it will mark the conclusion of one of the most important space missions ever.

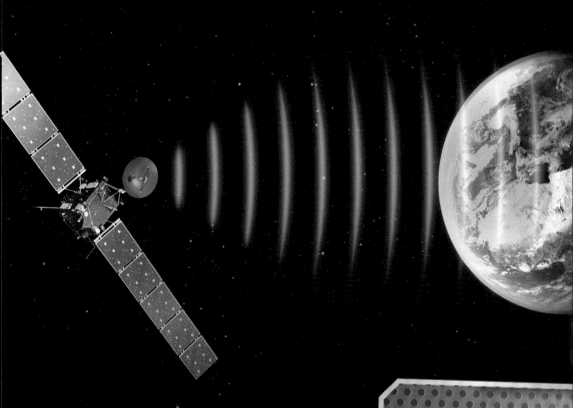

SPACE DISCOVERY

ROSETTA WILL CONTINUE TO GATHER
INFORMATION RIGHT UP TO THE
MOMENT IT LANDS ON THE COMET.
MISSION CONTROLLERS WILL KEEP
IN CONTACT RIGHT TO THE END, BUT
EXPECT TO LOSE TOUCH WITH ROSETTA
ONCE IT REACHES THE SURFACE. BUT
WHO KNOWS, MAYBE ROSETTA WILL
HAVE YET MORE SURPRISES FOR US!

Scientists
on Earth will
continue to
communicate
with *Rosetta*
for as long
as possible.

GLOSSARY

antenna A device for sending and receiving radio waves.

asteroid A large lump of rock in space. Many orbit the sun in a band between Mars and Jupiter.

atmosphere A layer of gases that surround a planet or moon.

comets Objects made of ice, dust, and rock that orbit the sun.

crevasse A deep crack.

data Information.

flybys When spacecraft fly close to a planet or moon in order to gain extra momentum from it.

free fall A descent powered only by gravity.

gravity assist The technique of using a planet's gravity to change the speed and direction of a spacecraft.

hibernation A state in which all nonessential systems in a spacecraft are switched off temporarily to save energy.

molecules The smallest amounts of chemical compounds that can exist.

nucleus The main solid part of a comet.

Oort cloud The outermost region of the solar system.

orbit To travel around an object in a circular way.

orbiter A spacecraft that travels through space, but does not land.

parking orbit A temporary orbit around Earth followed before a space probe sets off for deep space.

particles Tiny pieces of matter.

perihelion The point in the orbit of a comet, planet, or other space object at which it is closest to the sun.

probe A robot that is programmed to explore a particular area of space.

propulsion system A system that gives a driving force to push an object in a certain direction, for example, the thrusters on a spacecraft.

robot A machine that is programmed to carry out particular jobs.

solar panels Devices that convert the energy of sunlight into electricity.

FOR MORE INFORMATION

Books

Hughes, Catherine D. *National Geographic LIttle Kids First Big Book of Space*. Washington, D.C.: National Geographic Books, 2012.

Knowledge Encyclopedia: Space! New York, NY: DK Children, 2015.

Silverman, Buffy. *Exploring Dangers in Space: Asteroids, Space Junk, and More*. Minneapolis, MN: Lerner Publishing, 2012.

Stott, Carole. *Space Exploration* (DK Eyewitness). New York, NY: DK Children, 2014.

Websites

Due to the changing nature of Internet links, PowerKids Press has developed an online list of websites related to the subject of this book. This site is updated regularly. Please use this link to access the list: **www.powerkidslinks.com/res/rosetta**

INDEX